come Down, GOLDen

Diana Noonan

Published by Pearson Education Limited, Edinburgh Gate, Harlow, Essex, CM20 2JE
Registered company number: 872828

www.pearsonschools.co.uk

First published by Pearson
a division of Pearson New Zealand Ltd
67 Apollo Drive, Rosedale, North Shore 0632, New Zealand
Associated companies throughout the world

Text © Pearson 2011

Page Layout and Cover Design: Mark Glover
Illustrations: Renée Nault

The right of Diana Noonan to be identified as author of this work has been asserted
by her in accordance with the Copyright, Designs and Patents Act 1988.

First published 2011
This edition published 2012

2023
14

British Library Cataloguing in Publication Data
A catalogue record for this book is available from the British Library

ISBN 978-0-4350-7580-4

Printed in Great Britain by Ashford Colour Press Ltd.

Acknowledgements
We would like to thank the children and teachers of Bangor Central Integrated
Primary School, NI; Bishop Henderson C of E Primary School, Somerset; Brookside
Community Primary School, Somerset; Cheddington Combined School,
Buckinghamshire; Cofton Primary School, Birmingham; Dair House Independent
School, Buckinghamshire; Deal Parochial School, Kent; Lawthorn Primary School,
North Ayrshire; Newbold Riverside Primary School, Rugby and Windmill Primary
School, Oxford for their invaluable help in the development and trialling of the Bug
Club resources.

Every effort has been made to contact copyright holders of material reproduced in
this book. Any omissions will be rectified in subsequent printings if notice is given
to the publishers.

A division of Pearson New Zealand Ltd

Contents

Chapter 1
Dreaming of Dogs

"Monty! Monty! Come back here! *Monty!*"

From somewhere behind him, Louis heard the rough scuff of autumn leaves as something bounded towards him across the park. The closer the sounds came, the more the man by the pond shouted.

It would be a dog, Louis was certain of it. The quiet whirr and click of his electric wheelchair always excited them. Then they'd come racing towards him, sniffing the chair's tyres or running round and round in wide circles. Louis wished he could swivel around to see what kind of dog it was, but the padded brace that held his head steady and pointed straight ahead made it impossible.

"Monty! Bad dog! Come *here!*"

Mum's head popped up from the fence around the little kids' playground. Louis could see the look of panic on her face, which meant the dog *was* a big one.

Poor Mum, she'd been pushing Annabelle on a roundabout and now she thought she had to run to help him.

"It's all right, Louis!" she called. "I'm coming."

Now the man had seen Mum, too. "I'm *so sorry!*" he called as they both began running towards Louis. "Monty won't hurt him, honestly."

Louis opened his mouth and laughed as a huge golden dog bounded up to him and lashed his arm with its tail. By the time he'd managed to lower his chin to look down, the Labrador was pushing its wet nose against his hand and licking his fingers.

"Monty!" The man arrived, panting, and tugged the dog back.

"You really shouldn't have dogs off the leash in the park," said Mum, out of breath. She had Annabelle tucked under her arm. "It says so on the gates."

"I'm very sorry," said the man, snapping a lead onto the dog's collar. "I don't know what's got into him today. He just took off. I wonder if he might have seen that monkey."

"Monkey!" squealed Annabelle.

"What monkey is this?" asked Mum.

"Haven't you heard? A monkey escaped from the zoo last evening. Swam a moat or something. They're still searching for it."

Louis looked down at Monty sitting quietly beside the man's legs. His great pink tongue hung out one side of his mouth and his eyes were as bright as glass. He looked very pleased with himself for having run away.

"I'm okay," Louis told Mum. "I like him."

"What did he say?" asked the man.

"He said he likes your dog," explained Mum, who was starting to calm down. "Louis is crazy over animals and he loves dogs more than anything, don't you, Louis?"

Louis tried to answer, but his head had begun jerking this way and that against its brace.

"We don't have a dog ourselves," he heard Mum telling the man, "but we do have a goldfish. They're smarter than people think, you know."

Mum and the man talked for a while longer but, by the time Louis' head had decided to keep still, Monty was tugging on his lead and the man was saying goodbye.

"Brrr," said Mum, as they headed for home. "It feels like winter is just around the corner. I hope they catch that little monkey before it gets any colder."

That evening, while Annabelle watched her favourite DVD, Louis made a start on his homework. But his mind kept wandering back to the Labrador in the park. It wasn't fair that Mum wouldn't let him have a dog. It didn't have to be a big one like Monty. Even a little dog would do – as long as it was smart. Then he'd be able to train it.

"Have you started that homework?" asked Mum. She was sitting at the table behind him, typing on her laptop. She had eyes in the back of her head.

Rabbits were useless pets, thought Louis. So were guinea pigs. They weren't smart enough to get used to the sudden jerks and twists that his body kept making. At school, his class had a rabbit and even a twitch of Louis' head had it running off to hide in its box.

"I mean it, Louis," warned Mum. "I don't care if school holidays *are* only a week away. If Mrs Smythe has set homework, you must do it."

The chime from her email inbox ended the lecture. Reluctantly, Louis touched the "maths" folder on the screen of his Matrovix communicator. Then, a moment later, an outburst from Mum interrupted him.

"Oh, what!" she wailed. "I don't believe this!"

"What?" asked Louis.

"Dad's just emailed. He's not going to be home in the first week of the holidays. He's got a big commission and he has to fly to visit a couple who want their portraits painted. He says he's going to chat to you online in a few minutes to explain everything."

Louis turned his chair so that he was facing Mum. She looked really worried. She'd been working for months on the plans for a new mall and she'd set aside the holidays to finish them off. Annabelle was going to Gran's and Louis was supposed to be flying to Dad's, as he always did in the holidays.

"You can still get your work finished," said Louis. "I can look after myself."

Mum didn't seem so sure. "Maybe there's a school-holiday programme you can go to," she said. "That would be fun."

Louis moved his chair back to his communicator. Sometimes, when he had something really important to say, it was easier to use the screen than to waste time trying to make the words come out of his mouth clearly. He touched his "hobbies" folder and started pointing at one word after another as fast as he could.

When he'd finished, Mum let out a big sigh. "I've told you before, Louis, a dog is impossible. Even if you do have all the holidays to train it, I just haven't got time to look after it."

"*I* can look after it," Louis told her.

"And what about walks? A dog needs a good long walk every day."

Louis started to say something else but his video chat was ringing on the computer.

"Hey there, buddy," said Dad, in a voice that was trying to be chirpy. "Caught any monkeys lately?"

"What?" asked Louis grumpily.

"Monkeys. Haven't you been watching the news?"

"Dad," said Louis, "why can't I have a dog?"

Chapter 2
Tap, Tap, Tap

That night, after Mum had helped him into bed and gone downstairs again to work on her computer, Louis lay back on his pillows and tried to sleep. It was hopeless. All he could think about was a dog. Mum just didn't seem to understand what it would mean to him to have one. He tried to explain it to himself but it wasn't easy.

Having a dog would be like … like being on the back of one of the horses at the Equality Riding sessions he went to every month. When he was riding, all he had to do was whisper a command and away the horse would go. Round and round the field, it would glide along as smoothly as a ship over water. And away *he* went, too, way up high, covering distance without having to struggle with the controls of his wheelchair. With just a whisper, he had total command of the beautiful animal beneath him.

It wasn't often that Louis felt in command of *anything*, especially not his own body. But having a dog, one that he'd trained to follow his commands, would be like riding a horse. It would give him a kind of freedom. *And* it would be his friend.

Dogs could do almost anything if you only had the patience to teach them, and Louis knew he did. He was used to doing the same thing over and over again until he got it right. A wave of excitement, like butterflies in his stomach, stirred inside him. Dogs could fetch and carry. They could bring you the TV remote or a book. They could even pick up a telephone, which would be brilliant, because Louis was always dropping his cellphone.

Some dogs could even learn to open a door. And, if they loved you lots, they'd always stay close to you. His dog would look up to him with big, dark eyes, a doggy smile and a wonderful pink tongue hanging out of the corner of its mouth.

Louis let out the breath he had been holding. Mum just had to let him have a dog, she *had* to.

Louis was just beginning to think of some new way to convince her when he heard something outside. It was a sharp tap, as if a stone had been dropped onto the roof. He lay as still as he could and listened. There it was again, and again. It really *did* sound like a stone on the roof, unless it was the start of hail. But it hardly ever hailed, especially not at this time of year.

The tapping stopped. Then, just as Louis felt his body beginning to relax into the softness of the bed (as much as it ever did), he thought he caught a glimpse of something dark on the windowsill outside. One minute it was there, in the gap where his bedroom curtains were not quite drawn together. The next it was gone, replaced by a little strip of moonlight that was slowly stretching its way into his room.

As the pale light rested on the walls, Louis gave up trying to guess what was outside and looked at the paintings hanging in his room. They were all Dad's work, except for the few that weren't in frames – they were Annabelle's.

Mostly, Dad's paintings were of people. There was one of Mum and Dad and Louis all sitting together on a park bench – that was before Annabelle was born. There was one of Annabelle in her fairy costume and a really big one of Grandad, which was extra special now that Grandad was no longer alive. And then there were some others – hills and lakes and a chair with a hat on it. Dad painted in watercolours, so everything had a pale softness to it, as if whatever he was painting had half disappeared into the paper.

Mum was always saying that Louis would be an artist one day because Dad was a painter and she was an architect. The holiday programme she was going to find for him would probably be an art class. He didn't care too much what it was. If he couldn't have a dog, nothing else really mattered.

Outside, close to his window, the tiniest of noises interrupted his thoughts. It grew louder and turned into a soft scratching. At the same time, a shadow flickered across the paintings. Could there be a cat out there? Not unless it had climbed up the big birch tree and then leapt across to the window ledge. No, it had to be something that could fly – a bat or an owl – but he'd never heard of anyone seeing those creatures around town.

The scratching stopped and a cloud covered the moon so that Louis' room was in complete darkness again. He closed his eyes and tried to imagine what it would feel like to have a warm, soft dog resting on his feet at the foot of the bed. The way it would wriggle, just a little, whenever it heard a strange sound, or when he whispered its name in the night.

Louis let out a sigh. Mum had totally made up her mind that a dog was out of the question. But it was just possible that Dad might be able to convince her.

Louis yawned and thought for a moment that he could hear something dropping onto the roof. He closed his eyes to concentrate harder on the sound, and when he opened them again, it was morning.

Chapter 3

The Golden Call

"Morning," said Jazz, opening the door to Louis' bedroom. "Wakey, wakey." He pulled the curtains back so that the sun streamed in. "It's another lovely day of school for you."

"*Not*," muttered Louis, who was still half asleep. It couldn't be time to get up already.

Jazz was always bright, even first thing in the morning. He was a university student and he came around every school morning to help Louis get dressed and have breakfast. While Mum took Annabelle to the little kids' school, Jazz walked beside Louis and dropped him off at his school on his way to classes.

"I suppose you've caught up on all this monkey business," said Jazz, lifting Louis out of bed and into his chair.

"Kind of," said Louis.

"Hey, how do you get a one-armed monkey down from a tree?"

Louis shook his head.

"Wave at him! Ha, ha! I heard that one on morning radio!"

By the time Louis had had his shower and cleaned his teeth, Jazz had come up with three more monkey jokes and Louis still wasn't laughing.

"What's up with you anyway?" asked Jazz.

"Mum says I can't have a dog," Louis told him.

"Gotcha. That's a tough one. I remember when I wanted a dog and my folks wouldn't let me have one. They got me a turtle instead."

"A turtle!"

"I know," said Jazz. "We don't talk about it. In our house, we don't even mention turtles."

In the kitchen, Annabelle was jumping up and down at the table and Mum was looking frazzled.

"Morning, boys," said Mum. "Annabelle, sit down!"

Mum looked over at Jazz. "Sorry, Jazz. I'm not having a good start to the day. Annabelle thinks she's a monkey and *I* didn't get to sleep until 2am."

"How come?" asked Louis.

"There was a lot of thumping and bumping coming from next door."

"I want a banana," squealed Annabelle. "'Cos I'm a monkey!"

"We've got new neighbours," Mum told Jazz. "An older couple. At least, I think there's two of them. I haven't actually met them yet, but my friend across the street said she saw a woman going into the house yesterday afternoon."

"So what was all the noise?" asked Jazz.

"I suppose they were shifting furniture," said Mum, peeling Annabelle's banana.

"Peanut butter?" Jazz asked Louis, and he nodded.

Jazz cut up pieces of toast and began popping them into Louis' mouth.

"Are you going anywhere in the school holidays?" asked Mum.

Jazz shook his head and the beads on his dreadlocks rattled.

"I thought you might be available to help Louis. He's not going to his dad's after all, and we're going to find a holiday programme for him, aren't we, Louis? He'll need someone to take him there and pick him up."

Jazz didn't have time to answer because, suddenly, Annabelle let out the most terrifying screech.

"Annabelle! That is *enough*!" warned Mum, but Annabelle wouldn't be quiet.

"Monkey!" she squealed, pointing to the window. "I see a monkey in the tree!"

"No you *don't*," said Mum. "Now sit down this minute or you won't be going to Gran's in the holidays." She picked Annabelle up and sat her firmly in her chair.

"Honestly," said Mum, "I could just scream. Ever since her father mentioned that escaped monkey, she insists she can see one. She even got out of bed last night to tell me that a monkey was sitting on her window ledge!"

"It *was!*" said Annabelle.

"There *is* one on the loose," said Jazz.

"Don't *you* start," warned Mum.

By the time Jazz had dropped him off at school, Louis was tired of hearing about monkeys. So he wasn't exactly pleased to find, at current events time, that Mrs Smythe had drawn a map of China on the whiteboard and coloured in a little section in the north-east.

"Now, can anyone tell me what animal lives here?" she asked. "And I don't want any monkey business while I'm waiting for an answer." She laughed at her own joke.

Martin Taylor put his hand up. "Golden monkeys, Mrs Smythe. Like the one that escaped from the zoo."

"Brilliant, Martin. You've been watching the news. Or did you read it in the paper? Yes, this is where the golden monkey comes from – the same breed of monkey that has escaped from the zoo. Now, log on to the Internet, everyone. I want you to find out as many facts as you can about the golden monkey and be ready to report back to the class in fifteen minutes."

Louis touched the Internet icon on his communicator and entered "dogs" in the search panel. He waited. It wasn't easy to keep an eye on Mrs Smythe at the same time, but, if she did look as if she was coming his way, he figured he could close down the screen before she got there.

What he found himself reading next had him almost squealing with excitement. The secret to owning a dog, said the text, was to choose one that best suited *you*, the owner. For example, if you didn't have much time to exercise your animal, a small dog would be best. In fact, some small dogs, such as Maltese and Yorkshire terriers, got most of their exercise from playing inside. They only needed a short outdoor walk now and then to keep them happy.

"How are we doing?" asked Mrs Smythe from the front of the room.

What's more, said the site, little dogs didn't eat much and some needed almost no grooming. There were even breeds that didn't shed their hair – that would suit Mum, thought Louis.

He scrolled down to the section on training. Now he thought he really *might* burst with excitement.

"Just five more minutes," called Mrs Smythe.

Dogs were even smarter than Louis had thought. Some breeds were so clever they could learn commands after hearing them just six times. And, even if they didn't get to practise the commands very often, they *still* remembered them!

"Louis," said Mrs Smythe. "You look as if you've found something interesting about the golden monkey."

Louis reached out to touch the close button on his screen but he needn't have worried. A weird, high-pitched squeal suddenly came screeching from Darlene Butler's computer. It sounded like a strangled opera singer.

"Well done, Darlene!" said Mrs Smythe with a smile, forgetting all about Louis. "I can hear that you've found a sound bite with the call of the golden monkey!"

Chapter 4
Jazz's Discovery

"Drawing?" said Louis. "You've enrolled me in a *drawing* class?"

"What's wrong with that?" asked Mum.

"I can't draw," said Louis. "I thought an art class would be painting, or making things with clay or papier-mâché."

"Dad says you're artistic, Louis, but that you can't go anywhere in art unless you learn to draw first." She kept right on talking so that Louis didn't even have a chance to interrupt. "So it's all settled. You start on Saturday. Jazz will take you there and pick you up. I've spoken to the tutor and she's going to arrange for you to have a special computer-drawing tablet. It'll be easier for you than using an easel or sketchbook."

Louis reached for his communicator and then stopped. If he cooperated and got in Mum's good books, she'd be much more likely to listen to Dad when he talked to her about dogs.

"Okay," he agreed. "I'll go. It might be fun."

"I'm sure it will be," said Mum. She turned to the bench and began preparing Louis' after-school snack.

That evening, there was a big report on TV about the missing monkey. It still hadn't been captured and there had been no sightings of it. Zoo staff were beginning to think it might have been killed by a dog.

"If you do see the golden monkey," said the reporter, "be sure to let the zoo know right away. This is the number to call."

A telephone number rolled across the bottom of the screen. Annabelle rushed over to Mum with a piece of paper and a crayon. "Write the number here," she said.

By the time Saturday rolled around and Annabelle had gone off to Gran's, Louis had found out enough information about cairn terriers to write a book. A cairn terrier was the dog he was after – small, super-intelligent, a "non-shedder" and very loyal. They weren't great with small children, but Mum didn't have to know that. Besides, that meant the dog would stick with *him* and not Annabelle.

"All set?" asked Jazz when he came to take Louis to the art class.

Louis steered himself out the door and down the kitchen ramp to the path.

"Have fun!" called Mum. "See you at lunch time."

"You don't look too pleased to be going to this class," said Jazz when they were out of Mum's earshot.

"I'm not," said Louis. He told Jazz about his plan to get onside with Mum before the dog discussion that he was going to persuade Dad to have with her.

Jazz nodded and started to say something, but, suddenly, he stopped. He was looking down at a stick lying amid the carpet of golden leaves that had fallen from the oak trees above them.

"What's been having a go at this?" he asked, picking it up.

Jazz was studying ecology. He was probably going to end up as a park ranger. In the meantime, he treated any twig or stick that had a chew mark on it as if he'd discovered a dinosaur.

"A monkey?" joked Louis.

Jazz looked at the stick more closely. Every piece of bark had been chewed off and there were hollows all along one side where something had gnawed into the wood.

"We'll be late," said Louis, as Jazz began tying the stick to his backpack. The next minute, it was Louis' turn to be curious.

"Listen!" he said.

"Listen to what?" asked Jazz.

"That noise."

Jazz straightened up. "I can't hear anything. Well, maybe it's some kids playing somewhere."

Louis concentrated. There it was again.

"That whee-whee sound," he said. "You *must* be able to hear it."

Jazz shook his head. Louis couldn't understand it. But then Jazz hadn't been in class when Darlene Butler's computer had played the call of the golden monkey.

Louis thought a lot about the missing monkey that morning – *and* cairn terriers. In fact, he thought about most things except the bowl of fruit sitting on the stool at the front of the room. He was supposed to be drawing it. How could Mum have got it so wrong? Half the art class were senior students who were cramming for their art exam at the end of the year, and the rest looked pretty boring.

"That's a brilliant outline, Louis," said Alice.

Alice was their tutor and she used words like "brilliant" and "masterful" every few seconds. "Now try a little shading and, when you're ready, I'll print out your drawing."

"Shading?" thought Louis. He'd spent most of the morning getting the banana to stop looking like a grapefruit and now she was talking about shading!

Just before midday, Alice asked everyone to stop work.

"Tomorrow, we're going to the art gallery," she said. "There's an exhibition I want us to see. And now, for homework …"

Homework! Louis couldn't believe it. The morning had been torture and now she was giving them homework. He was so over drawing that he didn't even talk about it to Jazz on the way home.

Mum must have heard the two of them coming up the path because the front door opened and there she was, beaming.

"Well," she asked, "how did it go?"

"I've got a drawing to show you," said Louis, trying to keep his voice bright, "and tomorrow we're going to the art gallery."

"Excellent," said Mum. "I knew we'd chosen the right holiday programme for you."

Chapter 5
Unexpected Visitors

"Look up!" That was the homework Alice had set. "Look up," she'd said. "There's a whole new world up there and I want you to draw what you see. For some of you, it will be tall buildings. For others, it will be clouds or the tops of trees."

Louis tried to look up. He was sitting in the garden after lunch with his drawing tablet on the tray that lay across his wheelchair. It wasn't easy with the brace that supported his head but, by wriggling a bit, he finally found a way to do it. And he liked what he saw. Though summer was long over, some of the leaves on the tall beech trees were still green. Others had turned yellow and, here and there, patches of blue showed through gaps where the leaves had already fallen.

Louis was just about to pick up his pencil when an unusually big flurry of leaves floated to the ground close to his chair.

As if that weren't strange enough, the next minute he heard a volley of squeaks. It was as if someone was rubbing polystyrene against glass. Before Louis had time to adjust the position of his head, something scrabbled its way down the trunk of a tree and hit the ground with a thump.

Very slowly, Louis moved his head until he was looking down. He'd spent the morning convincing himself that it couldn't have been the missing monkey he'd heard on the way to art class. But now, though it was almost impossible to believe it, there it was – a monkey, standing on the grass just a few metres away from him. Its shaggy, golden-brown coat shone in the afternoon sun and it looked at him with wide, brown eyes. A bump of pale skin protruded from each side of its mouth. It was *exactly* like the images he'd looked at in class.

There, standing in his own backyard, was an animal that belonged in a zoo – or in a mountain forest in China. It was so strange that Louis didn't think to be afraid. But, when it began to make its way towards him in a peculiar half hop, half walk, his heart raced. Monkeys could bite and scratch.

The animal came closer and closer. If Louis called out to Mum, if he made any sound at all, the monkey might take fright and attack. If it did, he wouldn't be able to do a thing to protect himself.

Now the animal was right at his feet. It pressed lightly against his leg with its warm body and reached up a small brown hand to touch the drawing tablet. Louis stopped being afraid. It was so curious, and its face was almost human. He wondered if it was hungry, if it felt lonely without the company of its troop.

The monkey began touching the cord that connected the pencil to the drawing tablet.

Louis willed his head not to begin one of its crazy jerking spasms, but suddenly, the little animal yanked the drawing tablet off the tray. The clatter as the tablet fell onto the ground sent the monkey galloping across the grass and scuttling back into a tree.

Louis let out the breath he'd been holding. The missing monkey hotline number was still magneted to the door of the fridge where Annabelle had put it. He turned his chair towards the house. He had to get Mum to phone the zoo before the monkey disappeared from the garden.

"Mum!" he called when he was inside the house. "Mum! Quick!"

Mum came rushing into the kitchen with the phone to her ear. She looked worried, but not because of anything Louis had said.

"Oh, dear. I hope Annabelle isn't watching TV. Oh, this is awful."

"Mum!" said Louis, trying to get her attention. "Mum, there's …"

She turned to Louis as if she'd only just noticed him. "I'm calling Gran, Louis. You know that little missing monkey Annabelle is so obsessed with? I've just been watching the news and the zoo staff say that, if they *do* find it now, it'll have to be destroyed."

"*Why*?" asked Louis.

"It's been on its own too long apparently. The other monkeys won't want it back and it'll be too wild for anyone to tame."

Louis opened his mouth to say something else, but Mum was talking to Gran now. "Oh, thank goodness for that," he heard her say. "I didn't want her to be upset. No, it'll be fine if you keep her away from the TV."

Louis turned his chair towards the door and went out into the garden again. The zoo couldn't destroy the monkey just because it had been out of captivity for a week. It wasn't wild. It had come right up to him. He had seen its little face, bright and curious, but also sad and lonely.

Louis didn't know what to do. If he told Mum, she'd phone the zoo. She'd believe what they said. And there was no way she'd let Louis outside when the animal was in the garden. If he couldn't go outside, how could he ever tame it enough so it could go back to the zoo?

Louis stopped his chair halfway down the garden path. Was that *really* what he was going to do – tame the golden monkey? But how could he, all by himself and from his wheelchair?

He felt the start of panic, and the next minute his head was tossing to and fro in its brace. When the movement finally stopped, he found himself staring up into the face of a grey-haired woman who looked as if she was waiting to talk to him.

"Hello. I'm Barbara, from next door," she said. "I was watching the TV news when I looked out the window and saw the missing monkey come up to you in the garden."

Louis didn't say anything.

"I don't think it's wild at all," she said, "and it seems far too sweet to be destroyed. I'm sure it can be tamed."

"Don't tell Mum," said Louis.

The woman couldn't understand what he was saying, Louis could see that, but she seemed to be waiting for an answer.

"Use your communicator," she urged, pointing to it.

When Louis had finished, she looked at the screen. "I agree," she said. "We tell no one – at least not until we've had a go at taming it."

"Louis?" Mum came out of the house. "Oh, there you are."

"Hello," said the woman. "I'm Barbara Muir, your new neighbour. I just popped over to introduce myself."

Chapter 6
Lost in the Gallery

"I do like Barbara," said Mum the next morning, while Louis was waiting for Jazz to pick him up. "She's quite a character. Very independent. I get the feeling there's no *Mr* Muir."

Louis liked Barbara, too. He especially liked the way she wanted to save Golden as much as he did. That's what they'd named the monkey yesterday afternoon. Barbara had watched Golden from her deck as she read, and Louis had watched from his chair on the lawn as he tried to draw. They'd tracked the monkey as it leapt from one tree to another. One minute he'd be in Louis' backyard, the next minute in Barbara's.

The monkey had come up to Louis three more times. First Louis would hear scrabbling from the trunk of a tree, and then Golden would come hopping across the ground towards him. Each time he arrived, Louis put a piece of dried peach that Barbara had given him onto the tray of his wheelchair.

Golden came right up and took the fruit without even stopping to investigate. When it was in his fist, he scampered away to a low branch of a tree to eat it.

"Ready?" asked Jazz, coming into the kitchen and interrupting Louis' thoughts. "Art class calls."

As they went across the park together, Jazz didn't say anything to Louis about the stick he'd found the day before, and Louis said nothing about seeing the monkey in his backyard. Until he and Barbara had tamed Golden enough to show the zoo that he could be handled, the less anyone knew about him the better.

"Did you do your drawing homework?" asked Jazz.

Louis groaned. In between watching out for Golden, he'd tried to sketch his view of "looking up", but it was hopeless. How could he ever draw a million tiny leaves and the web of branches that he saw above him? His jerky movements weren't made for drawing. One minute he'd be concentrating on the curve of a leaf. The next, his hand would have a life of its own, dragging the pencil wildly across the tablet in crazy scribbles. He'd spent most of the afternoon trying to erase the few ragged lines he'd managed to draw.

Alice was waiting for everyone inside the art gallery when Jazz dropped Louis off. She had a gallery guide named Mirren with her.

"The drawing exhibition is on the first floor," said Mirren with a smile. "Take the stairs to your right. Louis and I will meet you up there." She looked at Louis. "The lift is right over here."

When the door of the lift opened at the first floor, Mirren glanced around.

"Oh, no," she said. "Where are they? They must have taken a wrong turn. You go ahead down that corridor, Louis. I'll find the rest of the group and we'll catch up to you shortly." She walked away briskly.

At the end of the corridor, when the others still hadn't appeared, Louis turned into a gallery. He knew right away it wasn't where he was supposed to be. It was a gallery of paintings, and he was the only person in it.

He wheeled his chair towards the door at the other end, looking at the artworks as he went. Some were of old-fashioned men and women having picnics. Others were of fields of flowers, a garden or a lake surrounded by trees. Though they were all different, there was also something similar about them.

Louis stopped his chair, and then moved in for a closer look. The painting in front of him was made up of hundreds of tiny dabs of colour. He moved along to another painting, and another, and found they were the same.

In the next, which was of a garden, dabs of yellow and orange, blue and purple made up the petals of just one flower.

Louis liked the paintings. He especially liked the way the dabs of colour could be used to make patches of light and dark. It reminded him of what he'd seen yesterday as he'd looked up into the trees. There had been dark patches where the leaves were still green and light patches where they'd turned orange and red, and where the blue of the sky peeped through.

He could paint like that – a dab of colour here, another there. There would be no need to be quite as careful as you had to be with a pencil.

Excitement stirred in Louis' stomach – the same sort of excitement he felt when he thought about training a dog, or taming a lost monkey.

He wheeled himself up close to some more of the paintings. This was the way he wanted to put things on paper. Not with the straight line of a pencil but with tiny spots of colour that shimmered and glowed and ran into one another.

"Louis? Found you at last!" It was Mirren. "The rest of the group is looking at the exhibition." She laughed. "I didn't think it was possible for so many people to get lost in such a short time!"

Chapter 7
Time is Running Out

After the gallery, Jazz and Louis had lunch in town. When they arrived home, Barbara was with Mum in the kitchen.

"How did the tour go?" Mum asked.

"I need some paints," he told her, "and a brush. And paper."

"I thought you were supposed to be drawing," said Mum suspiciously.

"*I* have some paints you could have," offered Barbara. She laughed. "I once fancied myself as a painter, but it wasn't to be."

Mum looked uncomfortable, as if she wanted to object but didn't like to.

"We don't want to bother you," she began, but Barbara interrupted.

"I'm going home now. Why don't you come with me, Louis, and I'll get them for you."

Come Down, Golden

Barbara's house was still full of unpacked boxes. Louis navigated his chair around them and saw that she had already put things on her walls.

"That's my husband, Ted," she said, when she saw Louis looking at a photo of a man in a wheelchair with a golden retriever sitting beside him. "And that's his dog, Rupert." She began pulling tape off the lid of a carton. "It was my job to take Rupert for his daily walk." She looked up at the photo. "I miss the dog walks now that Rupert has gone, too."

After a moment, she pulled some brushes and a box of paints out of the carton. "Here they are." She squeezed a little paint from each tube onto the tray of Louis' chair. Then she taped some paper down beside the paint. "Don't forget the dried fruit," she said, producing a handful of apricots from a cupboard. "I'll be right over here, watching out for the monkey."

"Have you seen him today?" asked Louis.

"Oh, yes," said Barbara. "But he won't come to me, even for food. It's *you* he wants."

Sitting in the garden that afternoon, Louis looked up. This time, he *painted* what he saw. Fresh leaves became dabs of purple and green, and dry leaves were flicks of yellow and orange. And, whenever he saw Golden sitting in the branches, he used little dots of deep brown and red for the colours of his coat. Around the circle of leaves that were the treetops, Louis dabbed the paper with blue, grey and white for the sky.

As he painted, Golden worked his way towards him, scampering down the tree trunk, sidling slowly over the grass and then padding cautiously up to the chair to take his fruity reward. Once, when his clever little fist brushed against Louis' hand, Louis thought for a moment about stroking him. But he told himself firmly, "Not yet. That will come next."

When Louis' paper was almost filled with colour, and Golden had paid him five visits, Barbara appeared through a gap in the hedge. "More paper?" she asked, without commenting on his painting.

"Yes, please," said Louis.

"I'll take this one back to the house and hang it up to dry." She paused and looked up into the trees. "You're doing well with Golden," she said, "but we must make a plan before someone else spots him." She looked over her shoulder at Louis' house. "We don't want the zoo staff coming around to investigate before we're ready for them."

"I'll try feeding him out of my hand," said Louis, using his communicator.

"Do you really think you could get him to take food from you that way?"

"Yes," said Louis. "Then I'll try to pat him."

"I worry about him scratching you," said Barbara, "or biting."

"It's okay," said Louis. "He likes me. I know he does."

When Golden visited Louis again that afternoon, there was no fruit on the tray. He looked at Louis as if something were wrong. Then he searched under the tray and looked up again. Louis opened his hand to reveal a small piece of dried peach. Golden eyed it hungrily, hesitated for a moment and then reached out and snatched it. When he decided to eat the fruit on the ground, just a metre away from the wheelchair, Louis knew they were making real progress.

Golden lost no time in coming up for more food. This time, he seemed to know where to look. He gently touched the fingers of Louis' closed fist. Louis opened his hand and Golden took the fruit once more. He sat up, right where he was, almost touching Louis' leg, and ate it.

Louis loaded his fist again but, this time, just as Golden was about to reach for it, Louis' head began rocking against its brace. He wished he could stop it, but there was nothing he could do. Now, as the spasm shook his whole body, all he could think about was that Golden would be terrified. The monkey would never come up to him again. How could he ever train the monkey, let alone a dog, if this kept happening?

Slowly, the spasm subsided. When Louis looked around, to his amazement, Golden was still there, standing right in front of him. His head was on one side, as if he were trying to understand what was happening.

Louis was so happy to see him still there that he felt like crying. He opened his hand. The piece of fruit was still in it. Golden saw it, too, and hopped forwards to take it.

"You've *really* won him over," said Barbara, striding across the lawn when Golden had retreated into the trees for a break. "Given a bit more time and I'm sure you'll be able to pat him. The thing is, we don't *have* much more time. And how can we catch him?"

"A cage?" suggested Louis.

"It'll have to be a cage," said Barbara. "But what sort? And where do we get one?"

"We've only got till Saturday," Louis told her. "Then I'm going to my dad's for a week."

Come Down, Golden

"No time to lose then," said Barbara. "I'll go to the pet shop this afternoon and see what I can find. In the meantime," she added, reaching for the painting Louis had completed, "would you like me to take this one inside to dry, too? I have a feeling that you'd rather your mother didn't know too much about your painting just yet."

"Thanks," said Louis. "That drawing class is horrible. I can't wait till it's over."

Chapter 8
Unwanted Interruption

On Wednesday night, Louis lay in bed with his eyes wide open and his mind a jumble of thoughts. He'd spent the afternoon painting, while Golden watched him from a low branch nearby. Louis couldn't stop thinking about how easy it was to paint what he saw using dabs of colour. It was as if the jerky movements of his body didn't matter any more.

Barbara seemed to understand. In fact, thought Louis, Barbara understood a lot about him. Perhaps it was because her husband, Ted, had been in a wheelchair, too.

Ted had had a dog called Rupert. Louis hadn't forgotten about dogs. It was just that, at the moment, Golden was taking up all his time. Taming him took a lot of planning and patience. This afternoon, he'd gently touched Golden's hand, just a little afraid the monkey might scratch him. But Barbara was waiting close by, ready to help if anything went wrong.

Soon after that, Golden had let Louis lightly touch his coat, then stroke it. And then, as if it were something he did every day, he had suddenly jumped onto Louis' lap and looked him right in the eye. It was as if food wasn't all that Golden was after. He wanted Louis' company as well.

Barbara had bought a cage from the pet shop. It was meant for catching wild cats. Tomorrow, they planned to catch Golden in it, and they knew they only had one chance. If the cage snapped shut and Golden escaped, he'd be far too terrified ever to go into it again. Their hopes of saving him would be lost.

"We'll bait it with some food," Barbara told Louis, "and leave it on the grass beside your chair."

"And if we catch him, then what?" asked Louis.

"Then we phone the zoo and explain exactly what's been going on."

"But what if they …" Louis couldn't bring himself to say "destroy him".

"Oh, I doubt very much they'll do that once they hear how you've tamed him. And they certainly wouldn't think of laying a finger on him once the newspaper and TV have got hold of the story."

Louis didn't understand.

"After I phone the zoo," explained Barbara, "I'll call the media, too." She held up her hands as if they were framing a banner headline. "*Boy tames monkey!*"

She smiled. "It will make a great newspaper headline and an excellent news follow-up to the TV's missing monkey story. If the zoo *does* have any thoughts about destroying Golden, they certainly won't go through with it with the whole country watching."

Louis smiled. Barbara was *very* crafty.

In the morning, after a restless sleep, Louis woke with a nervous flutter in his stomach. When he returned from art class at lunch time, he was still nervous.

"Hey," said Jazz, opening the gate so Louis could wheel his chair up the path. "I found some more of those chewed sticks yesterday. They were lying right here, in the street, after I dropped you home. They haven't found that monkey yet, and I keep thinking that maybe …"

"Yoo-hoo!"

"Good old Barbara," thought Louis, as her cheery call from across the fence interrupted Jazz. Louis waved back to her.

"What's that?" asked Jazz, when she came over with the cage in her hand.

"It's a cat cage," she told him brightly. "I'm a great bird lover and, if I find a cat hunting in my garden, well, I'm afraid I'll be returning it to its owner in this contraption."

Jazz put down the bag he was carrying and took the cage from her hands.

"Mmm, I could do with one of these to catch ferrets," he said. "I'm starting a study on them soon."

"You're welcome to borrow it sometime," said Barbara with a smile. She looked over at Louis and winked. "See you after you've had your lunch."

Louis was relieved when Mum said she'd be busy all afternoon in her study.

"Just give me a call if you want me," she said, watching him go out into the garden.

Barbara came across the grass with the cage as soon as Louis was out of sight of the house.

"He's waiting for you," she said, "in his usual spot."

Louis looked up and caught a flash of golden-brown against a background of green and yellow leaves. When Barbara put the cage on the ground and baited it with a plump dried apricot, Louis felt like a traitor. He knew catching Golden was for the best, but he felt as if the cage was betraying the trust he had built up with the little monkey.

"I know what you're thinking," said Barbara, standing back and looking at the trap. "I don't like doing this any more than you do, Louis, but we don't have a choice. It'll be winter soon and, if a dog doesn't catch Golden, the cold definitely will."

She walked a few steps back towards the hedge. "If he does take the bait," she said, "I have a rug to cover the cage as soon as he's trapped. The dark will calm him down until the zoo staff arrive."

Louis nodded. It was all up to him now. He had to be strong.

Barbara hadn't brought his painting things over. There would be no time for that with all that they had to do. Instead, he picked up the pen of his drawing tablet and pretended to sketch. Right away, he heard the telltale rustle of leaves from above and a scrabbling as Golden shimmied down the tree trunk. Louis held his breath as the monkey skipped sideways across the grass towards him.

"Hello," said Louis.

Golden looked right into his eyes, then down at the cage beside the wheelchair. Perhaps he smelled the apricot in it, because he didn't check Louis' hand for food. Instead, he tipped his head from one side to the other, as if considering what to do next. Behind the hedge, Louis could just see Barbara, standing completely still, watching and waiting.

"Come on, come on," said Louis to himself. "Take the bait, Golden."

"Hey! There it is!"

Louis' head jerked up. Jazz was striding up the path towards him.

"My bag! I knew I left it here," he said.

But, in the next instant, Jazz wasn't looking at his bag. His eyes were fixed on the streak of golden-brown that was suddenly leaping across the ground and pulling itself up the trunk of the nearest tree.

"What the …?" Jazz stood in the middle of the yard with his mouth wide open as Barbara came trotting across the grass.

Come Down, Golden

Chapter 9
Last Chance

After Golden had been spotted, everything seemed to happen at lightning speed. One minute, Jazz was standing on the path with his mouth wide open. The next, he was almost dancing on the spot as he ran first towards Louis and then in the direction of the house.

"Get inside!" he shouted back to Louis. "I'll get your mum. And don't touch him, Louis! Monkeys can bite."

"Wait! Just a minute!" called Barbara, rushing across the grass, but Jazz was already inside the house.

She turned to Louis. "Wait right here," she said. "Don't let Golden out of your sight. I'll be back as soon as I've made some phone calls."

She rushed off towards her house, and then dashed to pick up the cage. "No need for anyone to see this. Yet …"

Come Down, Golden

Louis watched her go then gazed up into the trees, where poor little Golden sat hunched on one of the highest branches. Somewhere, a door banged shut.

"For goodness sake!" said Mum, running up to Louis with the phone pressed to her ear. "Get yourself inside this instant."

"It's okay …" he began.

But Mum was already talking into the receiver. "Yes," he heard her say, "police, please – and the zoo. Yes, you heard me correctly, the zoo!"

"I don't think emergency services include the zoo," Jazz told her.

Perhaps Barbara had got hold of the police first because, when the patrol car finally arrived, it didn't have its noisy siren switched on and a zoo van was right behind it. Following close behind was a car with *Daily Mail* written on the side and a van with *TV News First* on its door.

From inside the house, where Mum had insisted he stay, Louis could see Barbara taking charge of the group that was fast assembling on the back lawn. Everyone seemed to be listening to her as she pointed into the trees. Then, all at once, heads turned towards the house and Barbara was waving to Louis to come outside.

"This is too much, Louis!" said Mum, leaving the group on the lawn to come to meet him on the ramp. "To think all this … this monkey business was going on right in my backyard and I didn't even know about it!"

"They're going to give us a chance to cage him," said Barbara, when Louis was on the lawn beside her.

"He's frightened," said Louis. "He won't come down."

"What did he say?" the reporters asked each other.

"He said the monkey won't come down," Jazz interpreted.

"Let's all wait inside my house," suggested Barbara. "I'll make a cup of tea while Louis does his best to lure Golden into the cage."

Louis saw Mum was about to object but Barbara got in ahead of her. "He won't come for anyone else, you know," she said. "Louis has a special way with him."

Mum sighed loudly, but Jazz put his hand on her arm. "We'll only be a few metres away," Louis heard him tell her.

When Barbara had finally managed to herd everyone into her house, she came back with the cage and put it on the ground beside Louis' chair.

"It's not going to work," said Louis. His voice was just a whisper. "He's too frightened now."

"We've got to *try*," Barbara told him, and Louis nodded.

As Barbara retreated behind the hedge, Louis thought he had never felt so miserable in all his life. High above him, the little monkey moved his head from side to side, as if he were an owl.

"Come down, Golden," begged Louis silently. "Please, please, come down."

Louis didn't know how Barbara kept everyone inside for so long. The afternoon stretched on and on while Golden moved barely a few centimetres from his perch.

Then, just after four o'clock, when the sun was sinking low in the sky and the air growing cold, Golden decided to pay Louis a careful visit.

It may have been that he finally felt safe or that he wanted something to eat before bedtime. Whatever the reason, without any warning, he suddenly leapt from his perch onto a lower branch and scuttled down the trunk to the ground.

As the monkey sidled up to him, Louis opened his fingers to reveal a fist full of dried fruit that had grown sticky in his hand. Gently, Golden picked up the lump and popped it into his mouth in one go. He chewed rapidly, looked behind him, and then suddenly leapt up onto Louis' lap. Louis could almost feel Mum tense from where she stood watching at Barbara's window.

"Hungry, aren't you?" said Louis, as Golden reached out to touch his hair.

"There's more down there, in the cage," said Louis, as the monkey probed his empty fist.

Golden looked at the ground, then leapt onto the grass and circled the cage.

"It's okay," said Louis. "I'm here."

Golden looked at the ripe apricot hanging on its hook. Then he moved his shoulder inside the entrance of the cage. From inside Barbara's house, the cameraman refocused his zoom lens. The reporter from the *Daily Mail* fired off a volley of still shots. Everyone held their breath.

Louis knew he would never forget the violent clatter of the cage door snapping shut a second later, or the fear in Golden's terrified eyes as he spun around and around, looking for an escape route. Louis willed Barbara to come quickly with a blanket that would cover the cage and bring some calm to the trapped animal.

His eyes filled with tears and his shoulders began to shake. "They won't hurt him, will they?" he struggled to say, when she finally arrived.

"Over my dead body," said Barbara fiercely.

A woman in dark green overalls arrived. She lifted the covered cage and carried it away towards the zoo van.

"I don't suppose we could borrow your son for an hour or two?" Louis heard a voice behind him ask.

"What for?" replied Mum.

"From what we've seen this afternoon, he seems to have quite a calming effect on the monkey," said the zoo official, "and, right now, calm is what this animal most needs."

"Well …" began Mum.

Beside him, Barbara held a tissue to Louis' eyes and gently wiped his nose.

"Please, Mum?" said Louis.

"Well … well … yes, of course," agreed Mum at last. "I'll get the car." She looked at Barbara. "Perhaps you'd like to come, too," she added. "It seems as though you two have had quite a bit to do with this monkey lately."

"I'd be delighted," said Barbara as the cameras whirred and clicked. "Let's all follow Golden to the zoo."

Chapter 10
Everything at Once

It was after midnight when they returned home from the zoo, but sleep was still a long way off. When, at last, Barbara had gone home to her house, and Mum was helping Louis into his pyjamas, they heard the video call chiming on the computer.

"Louis!" said Dad. "Got you at last. I saw the TV news at nine. I tried calling but ..."

"We didn't have time to grab our cellphones before we rushed off to the zoo," interrupted Mum, looking over Louis' shoulder at the screen.

"So it's all true?" asked Dad. "You really have been taming this monkey so you could save it from being destroyed?"

Louis nodded. "Yup. And guess what, Dad? He hopped onto my lap again tonight at the zoo. After everything that's happened to him, he still trusts me."

"The zoo's asked Louis to work with them to help settle the monkey back into captivity," added Mum.

"*Golden*, Mum," said Louis. "His name is Golden."

A grin spread across Dad's face. "I'm so proud of you, Louis, even if you did take a risk by getting so close to him."

"Golden won't ever be able to join his monkey troop," explained Mum. "The other monkeys will never accept him now. But, when he's comfortable enough with strangers, the zoo is going to house him in the children's petting park."

"It's going to be my job to get him tame enough," said Louis. "But the thing is, Dad, I don't think I can make it to your place next week."

"The thing *is*," said Dad, "if your time's going to be taken up with zoo work, where does that leave the dog?"

"*What* dog?" gasped Louis.

"This one," said Dad. He reached down and lifted up the cutest, curliest little dog Louis had ever seen. "He's from the animal shelter. I picked him up today."

"But Mum said …"

"It's all sorted, Louis," said Mum. "Dad and I have been talking dogs for quite a while now. We know how much you want one, but, until this week, I didn't think it was possible."

Louis thought he might be going to faint with excitement.

"I just don't have the time to walk a dog," continued Mum, "but Barbara *does*. In fact, she's desperate for a dog. It's just that she thinks it's too late in her life to actually *own* one."

"But how's he getting from your place to ours, Dad?" asked Louis.

The little dog squirmed and aimed a lick in the direction of Dad's ear.

"I thought he'd go back on your flight as part of your luggage," said Dad. "But I guess I can air-freight him. How about I fix it for tomorrow?"

"Tomorrow sounds fine," said Mum with a laugh. "But only if this boy of ours gets some sleep. He's due back at the zoo at ten tomorrow morning."

"Better let you get to bed then," said Dad. "Sleep tight!"

Louis laughed. "No hope," he said.

But Louis *did* sleep. In fact, it wasn't until Mum came into his room waving a newspaper that he woke and realised it was after nine.

"What do you think of this?" she asked, shaking out the paper so he could read the headlines.

"Barbara's going to be pretty pleased with herself," said Louis with a laugh. "*Boy tames monkey*," he read aloud. "That's exactly what she said the headline would be."

Below the article, there was a photo of Golden taking food from Louis' hand and a small note saying "more on page 3". When Mum turned to page 3, there was another photo. Louis gasped. It was his painting of Golden sitting in the treetops, but it looked like something from an art gallery.

"I saw it in Barbara's house," said Mum. "She said she was so impressed with it, she had it framed and hung it on her wall."

"Did I really do that?" asked Louis, staring at the photo of the painting.

"It's very, very good," said Mum. Her face was serious. "Why didn't you show your paintings to me, Louis?"

"I was supposed to be doing my drawing homework," said Louis quietly. "Mum, I can't draw. I tried, honestly. But I can't do it."

"Looks like you don't need to," said Mum. She stopped, as if there was something else she wanted to say. "The thing is, Louis," she said, suddenly becoming very serious, "I've had a phone call this morning. Actually, I've had a number of phone calls, most of them from people I don't even know and organisations I've never heard of. They all want to talk to you about monkeys. Or rather they want you to come to talk to them."

"Really?"

"Really. But you can't do everything, Louis. And, right now, you have a monkey *and* a dog to think about."

Louis waited. There was still something Mum wasn't telling him.

She sat down on the edge of his bed. "Louis," she began slowly, "one of the phone calls this morning was from an artist. A very well-known artist who's working at the art gallery for a year on a scholarship. His name is Eugene Montrose."

"I know who he is," said Louis. "I mean, I saw some of his paintings when we went to the gallery. That's where I got the idea to paint with dabs of colours."

"He saw the photo of your painting in the paper and," Mum stopped and took a deep breath, "and he's so impressed that he's offered to give you weekly art lessons – *free* weekly lessons."

Louis started to say something, but his head had other plans and began twisting and turning against his pillow. When, at last, it had stopped its movement, Mum was crying.

"You are the most amazing person I know, Louis Summers," she said. "I really believe you can do anything you set out to do."

"Except draw," said Louis with a smile.

"Well, the drawing was *my* idea, not yours," said Mum.

Behind them, someone tapped on the bedroom door.

"Sorry to barge in," said Barbara, "but isn't it time we were going to the zoo?"

"Oh, goodness!" said Mum, looking at her watch. "It certainly is. Come on, Louis, let's get you dressed."

"Shall I make some toast?" asked Barbara.

"Yes, please," said Mum. "That would be a great help."

"I have peanut butter on mine," said Louis. He wriggled his toes into his socks, then stopped and looked out the window.

"I wonder what Golden's having for breakfast?"